HIDE TH

The tric ... ok are
not for ev ... pledged to
keep its co ... other clowns.
Have it read ... nd consult it continually.

THE GREAT MEDICI'S HANDBOOK OF CLOWNING

Illustrated by Jane Wilby

SPARROW
BOOKS

A Sparrow Book
Published by Arrow Books Limited
17-21 Conway Street, London W1P 5HL

An imprint of the Hutchinson Publishing Group

London Melbourne Sydney Auckland
Wellington Johannesburg and agencies
throughout the world

First published 1981

Set in 11 pt. Plantin by
Photobooks (Bristol) Limited
28 Midland Road, St Philips, Bristol

Made and printed in Great Britain

CONTENTS

1. Tricks and Trickery 9
2. Slapstick 31
3. Clowning and Animals 42
4. Music 53
5. Trips, Slips, Acrobatics and Pyramids 62
6. Juggling 74
7. Costume 81
8. Make-up 96
9. The History of Clowns 101
10. Putting On Your Show 105

INTRODUCTION

These are the tricksters, mucksters, jugglers, acrobats and entertainers extraordinaire of the Great Medici's Clown Troupe on their way to last year's International Pie-Flinging Convention.

If you have eagle eyesight, you may spot a small book poking from their pockets, hats and trousers.

This book is nothing less than the legendary work, *CLOWNING AROUND: The Great Medici's Handbook of Clowning*. This secret handbook, carried by all the members of the troupe and consulted continually, contains all the secrets of

Allsort – the pigtailed trickster

Cani and Loni – slapstick specialists and pie-flingers extraordinaire

THE GREAT MEDICI – *leader of the troupe*

their acts – gags, routines, tricks, recipes for custard pies (*and* suggestions on what to do with them), advice on using music and animals in clowning, tips on juggling and acrobatics and ideas for costume and make-up.

And as well as revealing the secrets of individual tricks and stunts, the handbook shows how to put tricks together to make up your very own clown show.

The gags and routines in the book, like the clowns in Medici's troupe, come from all sorts of different backgrounds and clowning traditions, often going back hundreds of years. With just a little practice there is nothing in this book that is too difficult for you to master.

So, welcome to the clowns' fraternity, and happy clowning!

1 TRICKS AND TRICKERY

A performing clown needs to have a mass of magic tricks and illusions at his fingertips. This chapter shows the Great Medici's troupe performing a dazzling array of such material, all of which you could work into your act. Learn these tricks before going on to such major operations as sawing the milkman in half or turning your grandmother into a frog.

LEVITATION

Lorenzo the Magnificent lies suspended between two chairs, covered with a sheet. Only his head and feet are showing. The Great Medici enters and, waving his wand over Lorenzo's body, commands him to rise. Slowly, and seemingly miraculously, Lorenzo begins to float towards the ceiling.

Unbearably pleased with himself, Medici walks forward, bowing and smiling at the audience. As he does so, he accidentally treads on the edge of the sheet covering Lorenzo. It falls to the ground. All is revealed – Lorenzo never left the ground. He is simply holding out a pair of shoes on the end of a couple of broomsticks. The two clowns flee before the jeers of the audience.

The trickery

Take a big pair of shoes and place them over the ends of two brooms. Set them up as shown in this picture of Lorenzo caught practising at home. Use a large sheet to cover the brooms and body. Practice lifting the broom handles smoothly, keeping the ends of the broomsticks level with your head. Keep your head back, looking at the ceiling, and the audience will be utterly taken in and believe that the body under the sheet is actually rising.

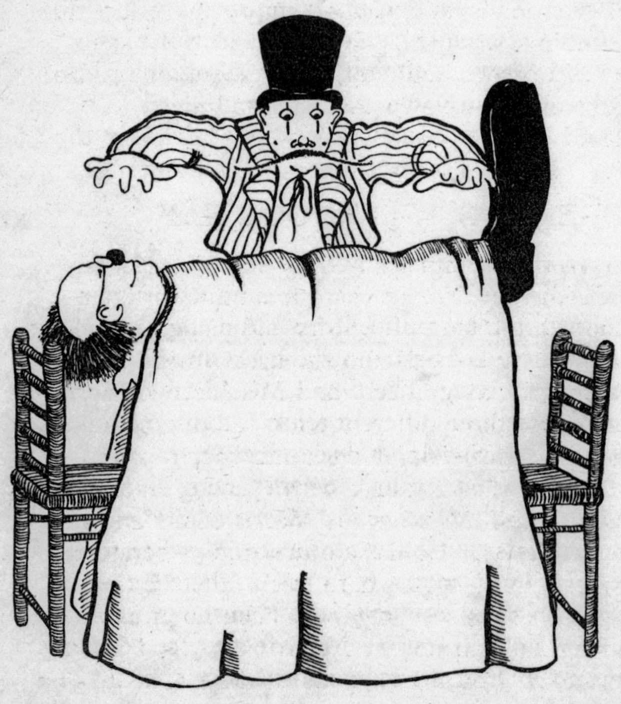

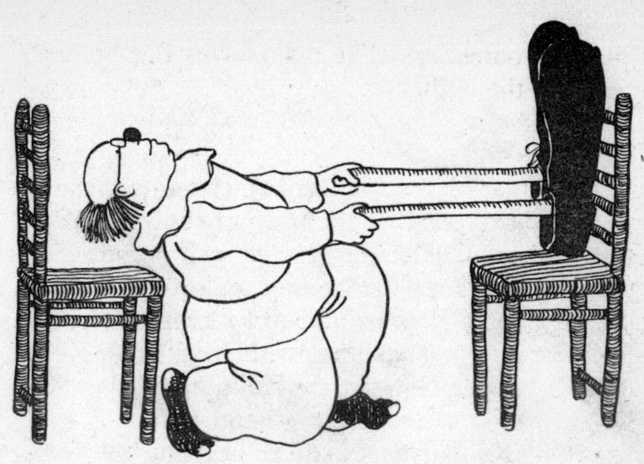

Levitation is an extremely impressive effect that is simple to arrange. You can use it in the same way as Lorenzo and Medici have here, or you can work your own clown character and ideas around it.

LORENZO'S AFTERNOON NAP

Clowns often employ the same sort of tricks as magicians but will use them in a quite different way, fitting them into a story and using their clown characters to elaborate on the trick. In this routine Lorenzo the Magnificent and Mischievous Morris Malloy use three different tricks, all of which you can easily perform and work into your routine.

Lorenzo is sitting on a bench having an after-lunch snooze. Mischievous Morris enters and sees Lorenzo asleep. He has a quick think – scratching his head – and then sets to work. First he ties Lorenzo's shoelaces together. Then he picks up the balloon, holds it just by Lorenzo's ear and jabs a pin into it. Nothing happens! Annoyed, he gets out

a big knitting needle and pushes it right into the balloon. Still nothing happens. Puzzled, he picks up the balloon and places it to his own ear. He pulls out the pin and sticks it in again. This time the balloon immediately bursts with a loud bang, giving Lorenzo such a fright that he dives under a bench for cover.

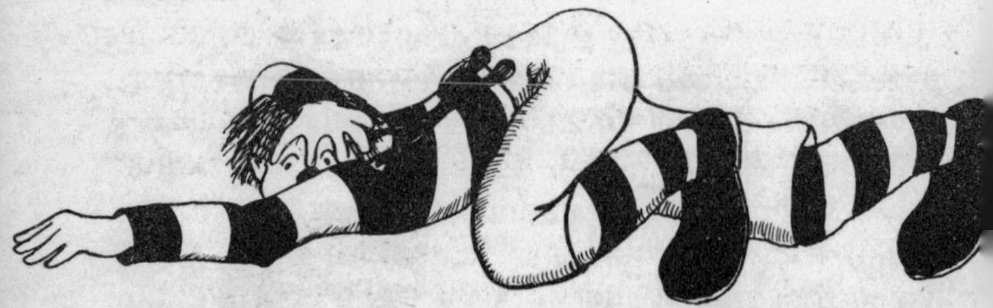

Meanwhile, Lorenzo still calmly sleeps on, totally unaffected by the events around him. Morris now gets back to his feet and looks around for something with which to get his revenge on the peacefully sleeping Lorenzo. Seeing a wand lying on the floor, he picks it up, puts it to Lorenzo's ear and pushes. Miraculously the wand slowly

disappears through Lorenzo's ear into his head. This still doesn't wake Lorenzo. It merely makes his jaw drop open, and there, across the inside of his mouth, can be seen the middle of the wand. Exasperated, Morris pulls out the wand. Lorenzo's mouth shuts like a trapdoor. Morris then tries sticking the wand into his own ear. This time there's no magic. Morris yelps with pain.

Now utterly exasperated Morris throws the wand down. Suddenly he has a wonderful idea. He marches off-stage and comes back with a custard pie. He takes a running leap at Lorenzo, but slips up and falls face first into the pie. Poor Morris! At this point Lorenzo wakes up, yawns, gets to his feet and exits without even spotting poor Morris lying at his feet. As Lorenzo goes, his shoelaces, that have been tied together, mysteriously grow longer

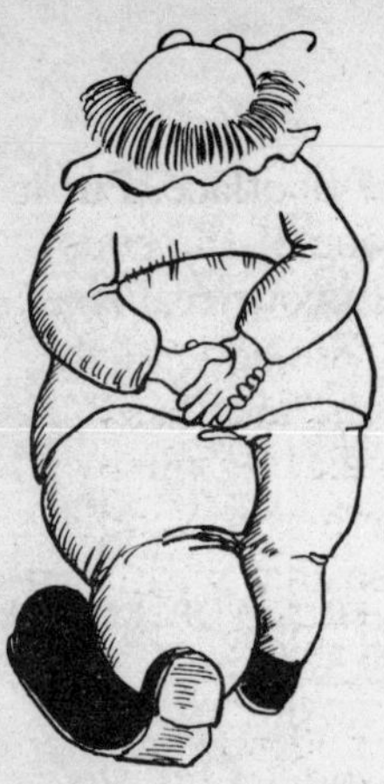

and longer. He's not even aware that they have been tied together. Poor Morris, blinded by the custard pie, tries to follow, but walks straight into a brick wall.

The trickery

Lorenzo's Afternoon Nap combines three different pieces of magic and a classic piece of clowning slapstick. All of them are tricks well worth keeping up your sleeve.

Pins in a balloon

This trick is simple. Stick a couple of pieces of Sellotape on to an inflated balloon. When the moment comes to stick the pin into the balloon, jab the pin sharply through the tape. The balloon will not burst.

Then stick the knitting needle through the sticky tape on the other side of the balloon. Again the balloon will not burst. When the moment comes to burst the balloon, remove the pin from the balloon and stick it through an area that is unprotected by tape.

Expanding bootlaces

All you need for this trick is a spare bootlace. Put it down inside your shoe and thread one of the ends up through the top lace hole. Tie up your real laces as usual but tuck away one of the loose ends of the bow and pull out a short length of the fake lace. Your shoes will look perfectly normal, but when your accomplice ties your laces together he should tie the fake lace to the other shoe, so that when you walk the fake lace pulls through and appears to stretch. If your spare lace isn't going to be long enough to allow you to walk, you could put another fake lace in your other shoe. And don't forget to make sure your accomplice knows which end he should tie!

The disappearing wand

For this trick you need a long, round piece of wood the size of a magician's wand. Paint it black. Cut two strips of white paper to wrap round the ends of

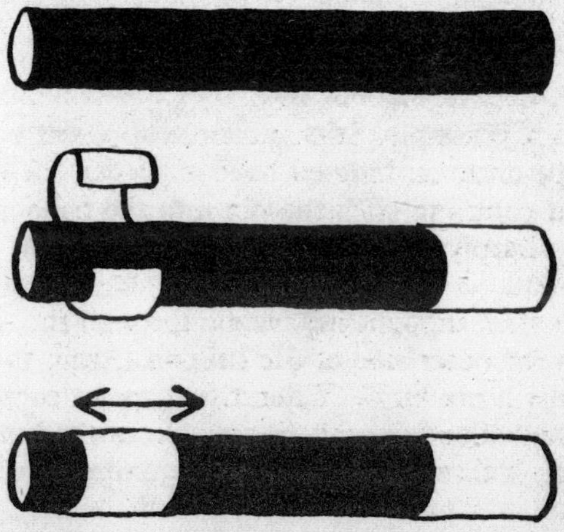

the wand and fix them on with Sellotape. Do this so that the paper will slide easily up and down the wand when pushed.

Take one of the white ends and hold it against your partner's head. Taking the other end in your hand slide the paper tube towards the ear, allowing the wand to disappear behind your hand. To the audience it will appear as if the wand is going into your partner's head. You must of course make sure that you don't really push the wand into his ear.

To make the wand appear in your accomplice's mouth, cut an extra piece of wood just long enough to fit across the inside of your partner's mouth and have it in place before the start of the sketch.

Tips on the making of really good custard pies can be found in Chapter Two, and for really spectacular trips and falls turn to Chapter Five.

CANI'S ROPE TRICK

Cani walks on stage. As he does so his trousers fall down, exposing a vast pair of spotted red underpants. Most embarrassed he tries to pull them up, but up they will not stay. In a real panic he looks in his bag, and to his relief finds a piece of rope. Unfortunately it will not stretch round his waist. He has another look in his bag and pulls out two more pieces, but they prove to be exactly the same length as the first one. Undaunted he folds them up in his hands and, praying for a miracle, gives them a good shake. He pulls out the first one, but to his horror it has shrunk to a mere 10 cm. He tries again. The second one has not shrunk but it hasn't grown either. Despairing, he pulls out the third one. On and on it keeps coming, so that

he ends up with a piece long enough to tie up his trousers and waddle off.

The trickery

Cani's rope trick is a useful trick to know. You will need some nice, supple rope. Dressing-gown cord works well. Cut the rope into three pieces, one of 10 cm, one of 50 cm and one of 90 cm. You may have to wrap a bit of Sellotape round the ends to stop them fraying.

Take the long piece, fold it in half and let the two ends dangle down. Now pass the small piece of rope through the halfway point so you end up with something like this.

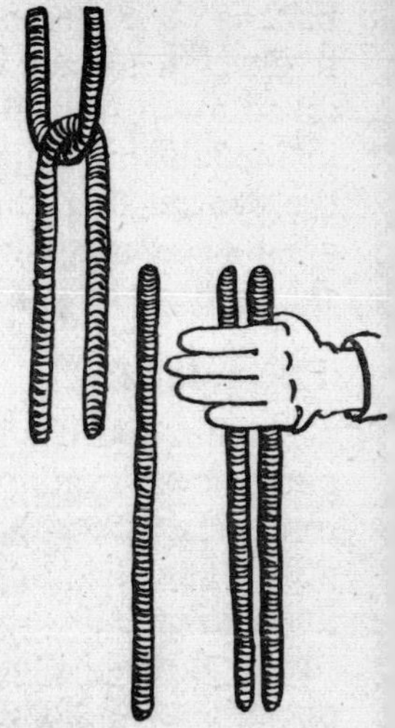

If you hold the rope at the point where they connect, hiding the join with your hand, the audience will assume that you are holding two ropes of the same length. If you follow the measurements given above these ropes will appear to be the same length as the third. It should look something like this diagram.

To do the trick, first hold the three ropes in your hand, as you've practised, so the audience assumes they're all equal in length. Then fold the ropes into your hand. All you have to do now is pull them out one by one, and watch the audience gasp. You can then hand them out to the audience to show that they are not made of elastic or 'fixed' in any way.

ALLSORT'S DEMON KARATE BLOW

Allsort does an act in which she displays an astonishing mastery of the martial arts. She tells the audience that her karate is so amazingly good that she can chop up a banana without even marking the outside.

First she asks someone up from the audience to inspect the banana for marks or cuts. Then with an almighty cry she leaps into the air, screams, 'AGHA WANG BANT!' and karate chops the banana. The member of the audience is then told to check it for any cuts. Not finding any, he's next asked to open it up. As he peels back the skin the inside falls out into three neat sections. Allsort takes the banana skin, throws it on the floor and takes a great sweeping bow. As she does so she slips on the skin and crashes to the floor.

The trickery

Get a pin and push it into a banana so that the point doesn't quite stick out the other side. Now rotate the pin back and forth and then carefully pull it out. The tiny pin-prick will be too small for the audience to see and the inside will be neatly sliced. When Allsort does this trick she rotates the pin in two different places to get three slices. When you karate-chop the banana make sure to stop just before you hit it or you'll squash the inside.

MORRIS'S MAGIC WASHING POWDER

In this act Cani and Loni come on with a big bucket of soapy water and start washing some clothes. (Lots of glorious slapstick potential here.) On comes Morris carrying two large washing-powder boxes, and asks them if they would like some of his new invisible washing powder, that not only gets clothes a 'whiter white', but even irons and mends them at the same time.

To demonstrate, Morris takes one of the boxes and opens the top and bottom flaps so that the audience and Cani and Loni can see right through it. Morris explains that it looks as if the box is empty because the washing powder is invisible. From his pocket he takes three dirty, torn old handkerchiefs, a piece of string and some clothes pegs, and drops them into the washing powder packet. He then closes the flaps and gives the box a shake. Finally, with a big flourish, he draws out the string. It has become a washing line with three beautifully clean and white handkerchiefs hanging from it, attached with the clothes pegs. Cani and Loni are dumb-struck, flabbergasted and amazed.

Morris sells them his other box for every penny they've got and hurriedly leaves. Cani and Loni are over the moon with excitement. They pick up an old tee-shirt and excitedly throw it into the box. They shake it just as Morris had done and then open it up and take out the tee-shirt. Written across the front is a sign saying, 'EVER BEEN HAD?'

The trickery

For this routine you need three dirty and tattered handkerchiefs and three clean white ones, two pieces of string, some clothes pegs and a magic washing-powder box. Never fear, for the handbook owner these are easy to make.

Take a washing-powder box, a really big jumbo-size one will do best. Cut out a piece of cardboard exactly the same size as the side of the box, and stick it into the washing-powder packet as shown in the picture. Because of 'perspective', the way the eye tells how far away things are, the audience looking into the box from end A will not be able to see your extra flap or the hidden compartment behind it. Before the show starts, put into the secret compartment the three clean hankerchiefs attached to a piece of string with clothes pegs. The rest is easy. During your act place the dirty handkerchiefs, and the second set of clothes pegs and string, in the box. When you are ready merely draw the washing line and clean handkerchiefs from your hidden compartment. To the audience it will seem as if the dirty handkerchiefs have been miraculously cleaned.

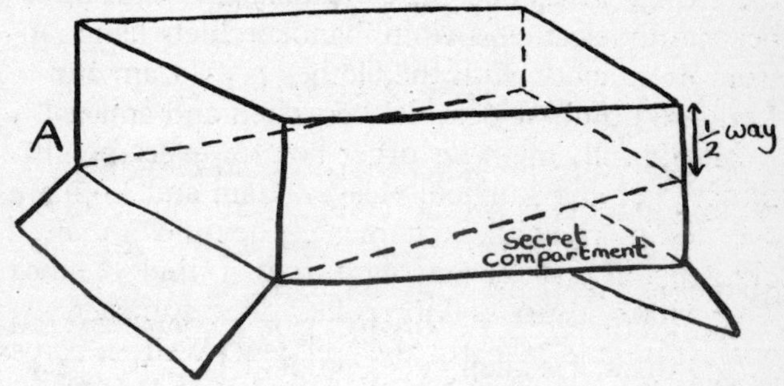

The final bit of the act presents no problems. Simply write or paint 'EVER BEEN HAD?', or your own punch line, on to the tee-shirt before you begin. When you place the tee-shirt into the box during the show turn the side with the writing on it away from the audience.

This is a very effective clown routine so practise hard and you will have a real show-stopper on your hands.

GRUMP'S BALLOON TRICK

This is a quick little illusion that you could fit anywhere into your act.

Grump takes out a balloon, blows it up and places it to his ear. He then places another balloon to his mouth. Suddenly the balloon in his ear begins to deflate and the one in his mouth to blow up, the air seeming to pass into his ear, through his head and out of his mouth.

The trickery

In fact all Grump does is to let the air out of the balloon in his ear at the same speed as he blows up the one in his mouth. A simple trick, but performed well it can get a lot of laughs.

THE VANISHING LADY

One of the Great Medici's most mind-boggling, stunning stunts is his incredible 'Vanishing Lady' routine. Hours of persuasion were needed to get Medici to reveal the secret behind this act.

Medici first gets Allsort to sit on a chair, covered with a sheet. He then gets Cani and Loni to bring on a screen and place it in front of Allsort. Mustering all his extraordinary powers, Medici shuts his eyes, screws up his face and chants,

'Do me a favour, Spirit of the air,
And remove this lump from this chair.'

He then asks Allsort if she's there. ''Course I am, you great lump of pickled lard,' she replies. 'Call this magic? My pet spider could do better standing on his head.' A trifle downcast, Medici explains that the screen must be getting in the way, and asks Cani and Loni to remove it.

He tries again, repeating his spell. Nothing seems to happen. A defeated Medici removes the sheet. To his utter astonishment Allsort has disappeared. There sitting in her place is the grubby face of Mischievous Morris Malloy. Flabbergasted he asks where Allsort is. 'Gone down the shops,' replies Morris. 'Easy when you know how.' With that

Morris wanders off. Medici hurriedly announces the next act.

The trickery

As always the secret behind this baffling piece of wizardry is remarkably simple. When Cani and Loni bring on the screen they drag it along the ground as if it is very heavy. What in fact they are doing is covering up the feet of Morris, who comes on hidden behind the screen. As Medici is saying his spell Morris and Allsort change places, Morris

being covered with the sheet. Allsort shouts out her lines from behind the screen and then when Cani and Loni carry it off she exits in the same way as Morris had come on. Simple, but a really effective piece of audience bamboozlery.

MEDICI'S SUBSTITUTION ENVELOPE

Medici's Substitution Envelope is a piece of magical apparatus that any self-respecting clown will find invaluable. What's more it is easy to make.

The substitution envelope has a hundred-and-one uses. It can be used for turning a £1 note into a £5 note, restoring a torn-up piece of paper, magically linking together paper-clips and all sorts of other marvels.

The trickery

To make a substitution envelope simply stick the fronts of two envelopes together. This will give you an envelope which will look perfectly normal to the audience, but will in fact have a flap and pocket on both sides.

To join paper-clips together magically, link up a chain of them before you begin your act and place them in one of the pockets of your envelope. Then when performing your routine show the audience the other, empty, pocket. Place the unjoined clips into it and shake it in the air. This will allow you to turn the envelope around without the audience noticing, so that you end up with the side with the joined paper clips in it facing them. Open up the flap and take the linked clips out, showing that there is nothing else in the envelope. To unjoin them just put them back in, shake the envelope in the air again, spin it around and pour the unjoined clips out on to your hand.

The same principle can be used in lots of different ways. If you know someone who would be foolish enough to lend you a £5 note, then you could put it in the envelope before the act and using your 'substitution technique' seem to turn a £1 note into a fiver.

To restore a torn-up piece of paper, place an identical piece in the envelope before the act and again, simply put the torn-up pieces in the other side and, without letting the audience see, spin the envelope around and take out the whole piece of paper.

HANDKERCHIEF PRODUCTION

Whether to blow your big hooter or wipe custard pie off a friend's face, a handkerchief is an invaluable prop. Taking a handkerchief out of your pocket is too straightforward for the resourceful clown. So how about making it look as if you magically pluck it out of the air? Magicians usually use silk handkerchiefs as these can be compressed into a really small space, but any thin material should do.

The trickery

Take the handkerchief, roll it into a tight ball and press it into the joint of your arm above your elbow. Now bend your arm. The handkerchief should thus be hidden by the folds of your coat or jacket. Keep your arm bent and it will stay there. When you want to produce the handkerchief first show the audience that your hands are empty. Then taking each sleeve of the jacket in turn, place your hand on the spot where the handkerchief is hidden and pull the sleeve up as if showing that there is nothing hidden up it. In fact what you will be doing is transferring the handkerchief into your hand.

Then, seeming to see something in the air in front of you, dart your hand out and produce the handkerchief. This will truly amaze your audience. If it sounds a bit complicated don't give up. Have a go. You will be surprised how quickly you will be able to master this invaluable piece of trickery.

MIND-READING THE MEDICI WAY

So far we have looked at various kinds of illusions and conjuring. We now come to something a bit different – mental magic. This mind-reading routine is one of Medici's oldest routines, and one of his real audience-bafflers.

Medici asks four people up from the audience. He gives them each a piece of paper and an envelope and asks them to write down who of all the people in the world they would most like to be. Then, without letting him see what each has written down on the piece of paper, he asks each one to put it in the envelope and stick it up. He then gets them to hand him the sealed-up envelopes.

To get his mind in full working order he gives his head a quick battering by way of a head massage. Next he picks up the first envelope and, summoning all his powers of concentration, mind-reads what is written inside it. He then opens up the envelope and reads out what is inside. Astonishingly he has got it absolutely right. He then goes on to work out what is written in the rest of the envelopes. The Great Medici is right every time.

The trickery

This trick relies on your having an accomplice, a secret assistant in the audience who is told what to write before the show begins. It is vital that the audience have no idea that this person is working with you.

This person should be called up with the three real volunteers. When you collect in the envelopes, place your assistant's on the bottom of the pile. You will of course know what he has written. Then take the top envelope and, pretending that it belongs to your secret assistant, seem to concentrate hard and very slowly chant out what you have told him to write. Then open up the envelope and pretend to read out the words you have just 'mind-read'. In fact you will be seeing what one of the real volunteers has written down. Take the next envelope and after suitable grimaces of concentration slowly chant out the words you read in the first envelope. The volunteer will be amazed that you have got it right. Open the envelope to check you are right and again pretend to read out the words you have just said. Of course you will be seeing what the next volunteer has written. In this way you will always stay one step ahead, always knowing in advance what one of the volunteers has written. The only thing you will have to be careful about is to make sure that the audience cannot see that what you are reading out does not correspond with what is written on the piece of paper.

When Medici does this routine he includes lots of clowning business. He pretends to get stuck on one of the envelopes, and has to tap the side of one volunteer's head to locate his brain. Not finding it there, he continues his examination only to find it in their backside. Because he always knows what they have written in advance he has time to think up jokes and gags about what they have written. As always this sort of clowning is what makes a really good routine.

PIERROT'S FLOWER PRODUCTION

One favourite trick of magicians is to produce flowers out of the air. Here the Great Medici's Handbook reveals how to do Pierrot's special clowning version of this age-old piece of trickery.

Pierrot does this routine without speaking, as a mime. He walks on with a big book under his arm, and holds a piece of paper and some scissors. He takes the scissors and cuts some paper flowers out of the paper. He then opens the book and places them in between the pages. He waves the book in the air, taps it on the cover and then opens the book. The paper flowers have miraculously turned into real ones.

The trickery

To do this trick you will need an old book, the sort of thing you can buy for a few pence in a jumble sale. It must be a nice large book, the bigger the better. Flick over about a quarter of the pages and then cut out large pieces from the rest of the pages,

leaving a one-inch margin around the edge. This will give you a square-shaped secret compartment in the middle of your book. Into this secret compartment place your real flowers before the show begins. You will of course have to choose flowers that will fit, so you will need a fairly small variety.

Before his act Pierrot also draws the outlines of his flowers on to his paper to make it easier for him to cut them out during the show. In his act Pierrot places his cut-out flowers in between the uncut pages in the front of the book. He keeps his thumb tucked into the place where his secret compartment begins (you could even cut out a little notch in the side of the pages to slip your thumb into). Then at the right moment he flicks the book open with his thumb so that the flowers fall out. When doing this you will have to make sure the audience don't see your secret compartment. Finally, you could gallantly present your flowers to a member of the audience.

2 SLAPSTICK

Many of the items in this chapter involve making a mess on a scale you may not have attempted before. So that a grown-up does not end a promising clowning career by attacking you with a rolling pin, always observe the following rules:

1. All pie fights, water fights and associated muck-making extravaganzas should take place outside.
2. Only clothes that are easy to wash, or very old should be worn.
3. Warn any grown-up who may become alarmed at the sight of custard-pie-spattered clothes of what you intend to do.

MUCK MISSILE NUMBER ONE: THE CUSTARD PIE

When a clown is given a tray of custard pies his first impulse will be to chuck them at the first moving target he spots. But if he is a clown who knows his business he will restrain himself and ask himself the question basic to all good clowning – how many different ways are there of using them and getting a laugh? Cani, when asked to ponder the possible future of a tray of custard pies, came up with the following seven ideas before falling off his seat with the excitement of it all. He thought of the pies being:

1. Eaten
2. Thrown
3. Sat on
4. Slipped on
5. Stuck down trousers
6. Hidden in hats
7. Balanced on the ends of noses

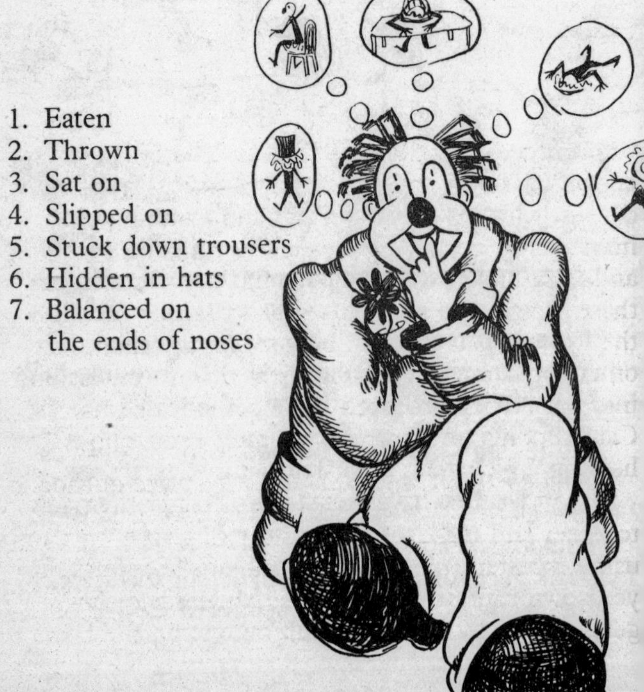

Inspired by his vision of the air thick with custard, Cani picked himself up and rushed off to consult with his partners Loni and Grump. They immediately got to work trying to think of a story and a routine in which they could use as many of these ideas as possible. They had to think up why the first pie was thrown, how someone came to sit on one and ways of getting them down trousers and into hats. They practised more complicated moves; Cani slipping on a pie and tripping Loni who is holding a pie which goes flying into Cani's face.

If you want to have a custard-pie fight then get together and make a list of all the different ways of using a custard pie you can think of. Then make up your own routine or story line. Maybe one clown gets blinded by a pie, slips up on one on the floor and ends up sitting on a third. Perhaps you aim one at the enemy and hit your partner on the back swing (this needs some practice) or someone ducks and you hit the person standing behind them by mistake. Possibly you could involve buckets of water and other slapstick ideas, or employ a few of your acrobatic or balancing skills. Once you've got everything organized and set up, make the custard pies and put your show on.

Custard-pie recipe

You can buy slapstick custard pie in aerosol cans from most joke shops, but it would be much better and cheaper to make your own. Get a packet of blancmange or custard powder and follow the directions on the side of the packet, telling you how to mix it up. To cut down on the cost of your pies, use water rather than milk and leave out the sugar. Ask a grown-up to help you heat the mixture on the stove. When you have made the custard or blancmange pour it in bowls and leave it to set in the fridge. Add a little food dye at this stage if you fancy having multi-coloured pies. Finally turn them out on to cardboard plates. You should now have some really top-class custard pies.

BUCKETS OF WATER

Buckets of water present all sorts of glorious possibilities for a clown's slapstick routine. They may be used for cooling burnt bums, be thrown out over people you have taken a sudden dislike to, accidentally spilt from the top of step-ladders over

companions, be used rather drastically to wash off a face full of custard pies, get stuck on the top of heads or become mysteriously attached to feet.

One age-old way to finish off a routine is for a clown to pick up the last bucket of water and, running towards the audience, slip, sending the contents all over the audience. To keep them happy it's best to put confetti rather than water in the bucket. The skill behind this most famous of clown gags is to pick the bucket up as if it really is heavy and actually has got water in it. Do this well and you will have the audience cowering under their chairs before they realize the trick that has been played on them. One word of warning: always use plastic buckets, as metal ones can be dangerous.

Cake-Making Routine

If you are hankering after a really massive mess, then this little number, the cake-making routine, is the one for you. Endless possibilities for sludge-and slime-slinging in an act that is a real circus classic. Here is one of the Great Medici's routines.

Medici is a master cook reading out a recipe to his assistant Loni. Loni, who is putting everything into a large bowl, gets all the ingredients wrong; flowers instead of flour, nuts and bolts made in Brazil rather than Brazil nuts, an electric current rather than a fruit one and so on. Finally, Medici tells Loni to beat the mixture, and Loni starts attacking it with a stick. Next, pushing him away, Medici has a taste of the mixture and pretends to swallow a nut that gets stuck in his throat.

Choking as if he is about to die he tries various ways of getting rid of it, ending up standing on his

head and getting Loni to kick him in the backside. Finally recovered, he gets up and tells Loni to stick his head into the bowl and fish out the rest of the nuts. Attempting to do so Loni gets his hand covered in batter, and trying to shake it off he splatters Medici's face. Medici has had enough, and a chase and muck-slinging contest follow which end up with Medici picking up the bowl and placing it upside down on to Loni's head. The batter runs down all over Loni and on to the floor. Medici creases up laughing, slips on the batter and ends up with his bum in it.

How to do it

Use a nice big plastic bowl or bucket. For your basic mess-making mixture just add flour and water and give them a stir.

Try working out your own cake-making routine. Here are some more gags you might use. How about cracking two eggs into the bowl and then slipping and throwing the third into the audience? The first two should be real, the third a plastic one which you can buy from a joke shop. If you are careful about how you take the tops off your boiled eggs when you have them for tea, you can save the shells for cracking over people's heads. Could you juggle with some of the ingredients? How about squirting some washing-up liquid into your mixture and explaining that it's to save on washing-up?

OTHER MESSY SLAPSTICK ROUTINES

Any everyday event involving water, paste or paintbrushes, food or other mucky substances can be used for a slapstick routine. How about a clown decorating team trying to put up some wallpaper? This would give you all sorts of wonderful potential for showing off your slapstick talents! What about a

clown window-cleaning outfit, or clowns working in a paint factory? (Of course you wouldn't use real paint, water with a bit of flour or powder paint added would be just the job.)

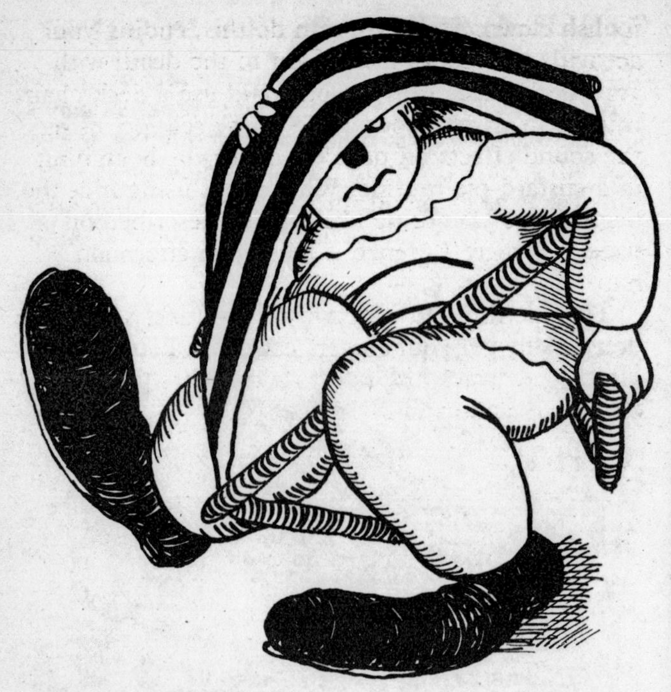

DECK-CHAIRS

Another clowning 'classic'. Get hold of an old-fashioned wooden deck-chair and see how many different ways you can work out of trying, but failing, to put it up. Now work out a routine in which you arrive with a deck-chair under your arm (maybe knocking over a few things on the way in). Start trying to put the deck-chair up, getting more and more frantic as each attempt fails. Begin getting your feet caught between the different struts, your head caught between canvas and wood. Really good clowns can make mere objects become like wild animals intent on trapping the poor, foolish clown. See if you can do this, ending your act with what looks like a fight to the death with your deck-chair. Maybe you could use a deck-chair routine in an act about a trip to the seaside, using the sound effects on page 61, or for the beginning of a custard-pie routine. What about using it at the beginning of a routine like the one described on page 11, where Lorenzo is having an afternoon nap?

The one thing to watch in this routine is that you don't really get your fingers caught in between the struts. As always, the safest routines are those that are slowly and carefully rehearsed.

3 CLOWNING AND ANIMALS

Animals are an excellent addition to any clown act, but they can cause problems. Apart from the expense, your family is unlikely to be keen on the larger variety. Monkeys have terrible table manners, few baths can accommodate a fully-grown seal and lions are not popular with postmen.

Household pets are of course a possibility. Perhaps your dog could do a few tricks or your gerbil could be taught to tap dance. But if you don't have a dog, your spider has no sense of rhythm and your gerbil refuses to concentrate, don't despair. In this chapter there are all sorts of ideas for the easy introduction of animals into your act.

CHARMING CYRIL THE SNAKE

Here we see Allsort doing a bit of snake-charming. In fact Morris has no cause for alarm. Allsort's snake, known as Cyril, is made out of corks. He dances because there is a bit of invisible thread going from his head to the end of Allsort's recorder. Up goes the recorder, up goes Cyril.

What you need

Make the snake by threading corks on to a piece of strong thread. (Invisible thread, which you can buy from most sewing shops, is best, but ordinary black thread will do.) Once the snake is threaded, use a pair of drawing pins for eyes and pink felt to make a tongue. Now tie a piece of thread behind the snake's cork head and attach it to your recorder. If you don't have a recorder a gazoo will do, or you can simply pretend to play on a stick of wood. As you play, the snake, drawn by the thread attached to the recorder, will rise mysteriously. A wicker shopping basket makes an excellent snake-holder or alternatively a cardboard box will serve.

THE HYPNOTIC EYES OF THOMAS THE TORTOISE

Here we see a picture of Cani and an old companion of his, Thomas, a very rare breed of the lesser-spotted Amazonian tortoise. To those not in the know, Thomas might look like a rather dim-witted gentleman. In fact he has the most remarkable powers of hypnosis.

In this extraordinary act they are assisted by Loni. Four people are invited up from the audience to be hypnotized. One by one they have to stare into Thomas's eyes. Then Cani gives them a piece of paper resting on a clipboard, on which they are asked to write down the first number under a thousand which comes into their heads. When they have all written down a number they are asked to sit down. Another member of the audience is then invited up to add together all the numbers and read out the total.

After this Thomas withdraws into his shell for a moment and comes out with a sealed envelope in his mouth. Inside the envelope there is found the exact number that has just been read out, the total of the four numbers written down by the audience. Impossible? Not for the owner of this handbook.

How it is done

The secret behind this baffling brain-teaser of an act is remarkably simple. As the four volunteers are sitting down, Loni, careful that the audience cannot see, turns over the piece of paper on which the numbers are written. On the back is a second list of figures that he wrote down before the show (remembering to use four different sorts of handwriting) the total of which has been added up and put in Thomas's shell before the start of the show. It is these figures that the member of the audience adds up.

How to make Thomas the tortoise

Make the shell out of papier mâché. Use the method as for the bald head on page 83, but instead of using a balloon use a large mixing bowl. Smear the outside of the bowl with vaseline. Then layer the paper over the bowl until you get the approximate shape of a tortoise shell. Leave it to dry overnight.

Remove the shell from the bowl. Put it on a sheet of card and draw round it. Cut out this shape to use as your base. Then cut two semicircles out of the shell at each end large enough for your arm to pass through. Finally, stick the shell to the base with some more papier mâché. Paint the shell and maybe varnish it.

Cut four short lengths of thick rope or cord, and stick them on as feet. For the head use an old sock. Put the sock on your hand and make the mouth using your fingers at the top and your thumb at the bottom.

Stitch on buttons or beads for eyes and nose. With the sock on your hand pass your arm through the holes in the shell. You will now have a very realistic lesser-spotted Amazonian tortoise.

The routine

Hold your tortoise as Cani does, supporting him with your free hand. Practise making his head movements as realistic as possible. Try giving your tortoise an individual character. Maybe he is shy or lazy and refuses to come out of his shell at first, or maybe he is vicious and keeps biting your finger.

A Tramp's Best Friend

Look at the picture of Grump and his dog Bert on the next page. Before Grump sewed on three large buttons as eyes and a nose Bert was in fact nothing more than an old moth-eaten sheepskin rug. Grump leads Bert around using an old piece of rope as a lead. The two of them look equally bedraggled.

They do a routine in which Grump tries to get Bert to jump through a hoop. But his faithful companion keeps falling asleep and refusing to move. Grump gets more and more passionate in his appeals to Bert to jump.

Finally, he turns away in despair and is about to walk off when suddenly Bert leaps into the air, jumps through the hoop and flies into Grump's arms.

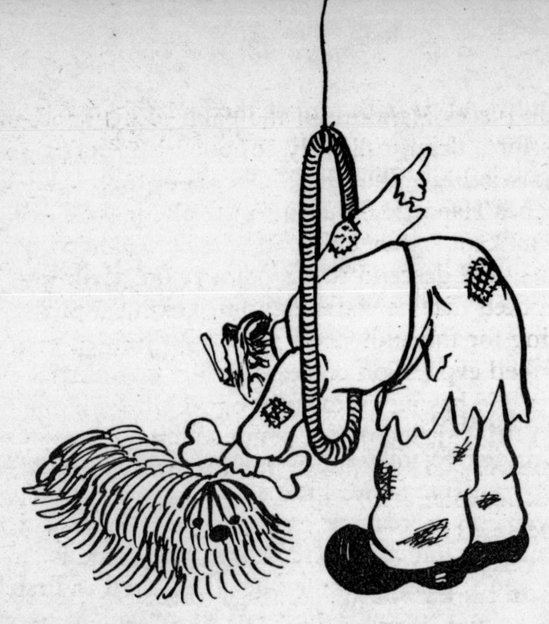

How it is done

This effect is very simple to work. Thread the dog's lead through the hoop and then suddenly tug it towards you. The dog previously so unwilling will now eagerly leap through the hoop.

The Great Hanratti

Grump's finest hour! He walks on stage and, with suitable dignity and awe, announces that it is his honour to introduce that Marvel of the Air, that Death-Defying Stunster, that Miracle of Motion – the Great Hanratti. In hushed tones he tells the audience that Hanratti is to attempt his legendary triple somersault with a left-handed back twist while juggling five balls. Then from behind his back he takes a matchbox, opens it and lifts out Hanratti, his performing flea.

He places Hanratti on the palm of his hand and asks for a drum roll, ably supplied by Morris on his percussion kit. Shouting, 'One, two, three!' he watches Hanratti fly up into the air, make three magnificent somersaults, all with left-handed back twists, and descend to his palm again. Grump is so delighted that he starts clapping enthusiastically, calling for the audience's applause. Suddenly an appalled expression comes over his face and he stops. He has just remembered where he last saw Hanratti – sitting on the palm of his hand. Frantically he starts to search his palm for Hanratti, or rather Hanratti's squelched remains.

He's just beginning to puzzle what could have happened to him when he notices that there's an itch on his leg and it's getting worse. His flea has escaped and is biting him! He starts to scratch himself, slowly becoming more frantic as he follows the trail of the bites, as they zig-zag across his body. Having just about scratched himself to pieces he finally catches up with the fugitive flea and, picking up him between his fingernails, places him firmly on his hand. He lifts up a finger to give him a telling-off, when suddenly to his horror he sees Hanratti take an almighty leap high into the air and down into the audience. Disaster! A desperate Grump runs into the audience and starts searching for the missing performer. It needs the entire clown troupe to pull him away and leave Hanratti to his new-found freedom.

How it is done

Of course the performing flea doesn't really exist at all. But if he did he would be too small for the audience to see anyway. It is the utterly realistic

way in which Grump pretends to pick him up and to watch him doing his acrobatics that makes the audience half-believe that he is really there. If this act is to be done properly it will need some practice, but if you master it you will be able to perform one of the most ancient and famous of clown routines.

ERNEST: THE WORLD'S ONLY CHEESE-POWERED ROCKET

In comes Medici followed by Lorenzo, who is carrying a box. With suitable huffing and puffing Medici announces that the box contains none other than that athlete and mouse extraordinaire, Ernest, who, fuelled on nothing but gherkins and cheese, has travelled at speeds of over 200 m.p.h. Medici opens the box. Panic! Ernest has escaped! Lorenzo screams and jumps on to a chair. Medici begins a frantic search, crawling under the chairs of the audience. Chaos reigns! Eventually Medici finds Ernest was in his pocket all along!

From his bag Medici takes a paper cup, puts Ernest in it, covers it with a hankerchief and places it on the floor. He then takes another cup, shows it to be empty and puts it down on the ground a good distance from the first cup, again covering it with a handkerchief. He then explains that when he shouts, 'Go!' Ernest will hurl himself out of his cup, rush twice round the room and dive into the empty cup, at such an astonishing speed that only those with the keenest eyesight will see him. Quivering with excitement Medici shouts, 'Ready, steady, go!' and with his head whizzing back and forth seems to see Ernest leap into the air, dash round the room and disappear just in the way he described. He shows that the first cup is empty and that Ernest has successfully made it to the other one. He asks for the audience's applause, and is just about to bow when Ernest makes a dash for freedom straight down inside his trousers. Exit Medici in a panic.

The routine

Unless you have a small and remarkable tame mouse it would be best to buy a felt one as sold in most pet shops. The smaller the mouse, the easier the trick.

The trick

The trick at the centre of the routine, making Ernest travel invisibly from one cup to the other, is very simple and can be used as the principle for lots of different acts.

Take two paper cups and cut the bottoms out. Hold the base of the first cup in your palm. When you put Ernest into it allow him to fall through into your hand. Cover the cup with the handkerchief and put it down. Pick the other cup up, keeping Ernest hidden in your hand. Turn it upside down and show it's empty, and then place the bottom of the cup into the palm of your hand, over the top of Ernest. The 'switch' is now complete. Cover it up with a handkerchief and you're home and dry. Practise until you can do it perfectly without the audience seeing the swap.

4 MUSIC

Music has always played an important part in clown acts and many clowns are accomplished musicians. If you can already play an instrument you are off to a head start. If not, never fear, for here is a whole list of instruments you can make and play yourself.

CLOWN ORCHESTRA

Here we see a picture of the Great Medici's Clown Orchestra. All these instruments are made with easily obtainable rubbish and junk. How about trying to make one?

Cardboard xylophone

The instrument Cani and Loni are playing was designed by the Great Medici himself and is called a 'cardboard xylophone'. To make one you will need 4 metres of string, 3 metres of thick cardboard tubing and two chairs. Cut the cardboard tube into

four varying lengths and string them between the two chairs as in this picture. The best cardboard tubing to use is the sort they wrap carpets and material around, so ask in a material or carpet shop if they could give you a length.

Play your instrument with wooden spoons or drum sticks. The longer the tube the lower the note, the shorter the tube the higher the note.

Tea-chest bass

The splendid instrument Lorenzo is playing is a tea-chest bass. To make one you will need a tea-chest, $1\frac{1}{2}$ metres of thick string and a broom handle. Turn the tea-chest upside down and pierce a hole in the bottom of it. Thread your piece of string through the hole and tie a knot in the end to secure it. Hold the broomhandle vertically, with its base resting on the corner of the box, and tack or tie the string to the top of the pole, without allowing it to slacken. You may need someone to help you do this.

To play your tea-chest bass pull the top of the broom handle towards you, thus stretching the string, and pluck it. This should send vibrations

down the string into the tea-chest, producing a note. Let the string slacken to lower the note and tighten it to raise it. With a bit of practice it's quite easy to play a tune on your bass.

Percussion kit

Morris's percussion kit is made up of all kinds of household bits and pieces, each of which produces a different sort of sound when deftly clunked with his wooden-spoon drumsticks. Can you think of some other useful percussion instruments that Morris hasn't included?

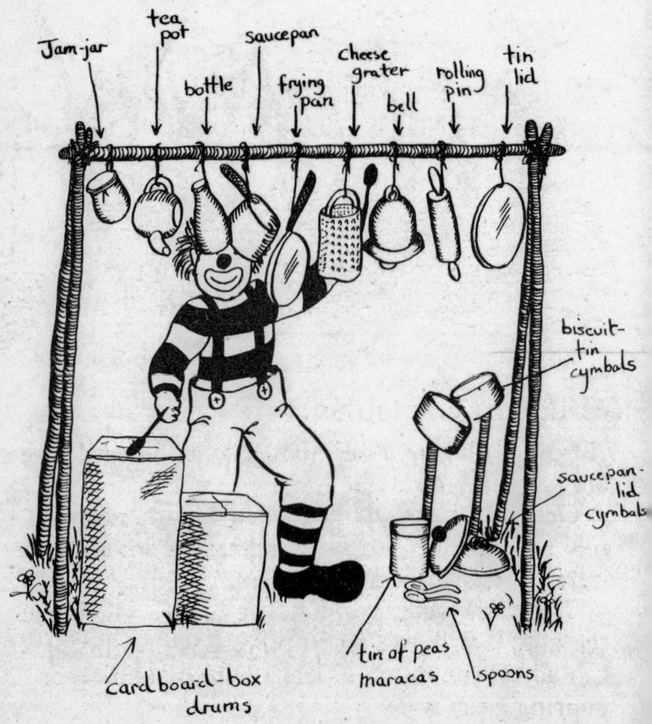

Swanee whistle

It's possible to buy a small bamboo swanee whistle from toy or music shops for twenty pence or so. This would be a good investment as these are extremely easy to play and produce an excellent clown sound.

Milk-bottle xylophone

Allsort is playing a milk-bottle xylophone. These are *very* easy to make.

Get eight empty milk bottles, line them up in a row and fill each one with increasing amounts of water as shown in the picture.

The more water you have in a bottle the higher the note it will give when played with a spoon. You can adjust the 'pitch' of each note by adding or pouring away water.

Gazoo

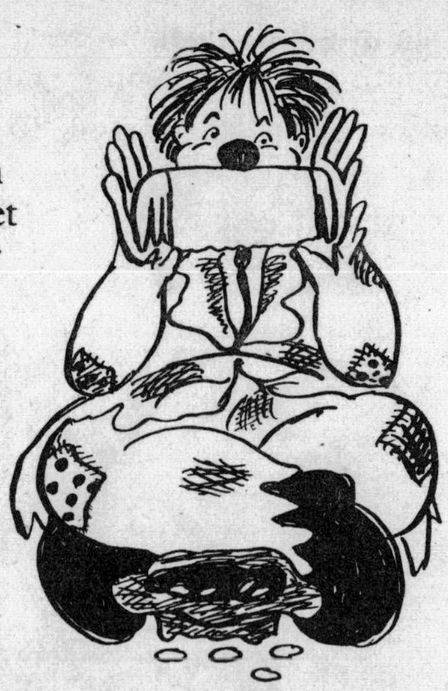

For this virtuoso instrument all you need is a comb and some thin wax paper or 'hard' toilet paper. Stretch the paper over the teeth of the comb, place it against your mouth and hum through it. Some joke shops sell huge joke combs that are not too expensive, and make really good jumbo gazoos.

PLAYING THE NASHERS

Nasher-, or teeth-playing is an ancient Somerset art. Open your mouth and tap your top teeth with your fingernail or a pencil. If you close your

mouth a little the note goes down, open your mouth and it goes up. Again, try and work out a tune. Easily popped into any part of your act.

SINGING WITH YOUR HEAD IN A BUCKET OF WATER

As this performance can be a little wet, it is best suited to outside shows. Announce that you are to give the world's first underwater performance of whatever tune takes your fancy. Set up your sheet of music on a chair just by a bucket of water and then, taking a big breath, plunge your head into the bucket and start singing, coming up for air to read the next lot of music at the end of each line. When Mischievous Morris does this act he starts choking in the middle of the song and comes up with a fish in his mouth (a carrot which Morris cut into the shape of a goldfish and placed in the bucket beforehand).

DROOPING CONDUCTOR'S BATON

Medici uses a conductor's baton which is able to droop and straighten depending on how much it's enjoying the music. To make one of these, get five corks, drill holes through the middle of them and then paint them black. Now thread a piece of string through the corks and tie a knot where it emerges out of the fifth cork. If you now pull the other end of the string tight the baton will look from a little distance like a normal conductor's baton. Let the string slacken and it will droop.

SOUND EFFECTS

The use of sound effects in your act adds a bit of razzamatazz and class to your show. You should be able to think of your own effects but here are some suggestions.

Crashes, bangs, larder-raiding noises etc.

Keep a large cardboard box of broken plates, bits of iron and pots and pans off-stage thumping up and down when such noises are required.

Horses' gallop

Get a couple of halved coconut shells. By banging the halves together you get a sound like horses' hooves galloping along a road.

Sea

Get a shoe-box and fill it with dried peas, covering about half of the bottom of the box. By tipping the box from side to side you produce a sound just like the surf at the sea-side. It might accompany a clown outing to the sea or the deck-chair routine in the slapstick chapter.

Wind (as in North Wind)

Get a bottle and blow over the top. With some practice you should be able to produce anything from a breeze to a storm. How about a routine about a tramp clown trying to get warm?

Wind (as in raspberry)

Place tongue firmly between lips and blow. Adaptable to a sitting-on-custard-pie sort of squelch and various other invaluable sound effects.

5 TRIPS, SLIPS, ACROBATICS AND PYRAMIDS

As a clown you will be doing lots of tripping, slipping and falling. This chapter will give you some ideas for making these a bit more exciting, as well as showing you how to learn and perform acrobatic and pyramid stunts. Unless you have a concrete head it would be best to practise these on soft grass or gym mats.

TRIPS AND SLIPS

The simple trip

Walk along and then pretend to trip. Keep your body straight as you fall, but place your hands out in front of you to catch yourself. As your hands come in contact with the ground fold them up quickly. Immediately start rubbing your head as if you've given yourself a terrible wallop.

Trip into a somersault

The first step in mastering this move is to do a forward roll. Crouch down with your knees together and your hands out in front of you. Place your hands on the ground, put your head between your arms and roll forward. As you go tuck your head well in to your chest so that the back of your neck touches the ground first. Now reach forward with your hands so that you return to a crouched position.

Your next step is to try this from a standing position, and finally walking along and tripping as if by accident. If you want to be really classy you could try it with no hands, maybe holding a custard pie. See if you can do it without spilling the pie.

THE BACKWARD TRIP AND ROLL

There are several occasions in the handbook when clowns, blinded by custard pies or by buckets over their heads, run into walls or other clowns. To give such moments a really classy touch, you could be sent hurtling back into a backward trip and roll. Backward trips and rolls can also be used for more common slips, slides and falls.

Start as in a forward roll with your arms stretched out in front of you. Fall backwards on to your behind, curl up in a ball and roll over backwards. As you roll, place your palms on the

ground next to your ears, and push so that your legs go over your head and you come back into a crouch. When you have mastered this, try it from a standing position. Finally practise making it look as if you are knocked backwards accidentally, before going into your roll. These trips and falls once learnt will be used again and again.

TANK ROLLS

A nice comical effect this, for two clowns. Start in the position shown in the drawing above. If you are the one who is standing, slowly lean forward. As

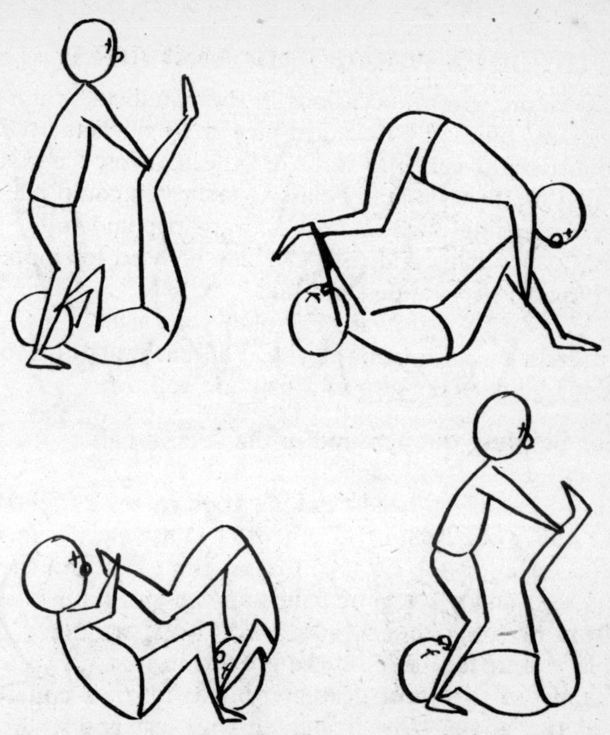

your partner's legs approach the ground move them apart, tuck your head in between them and roll forward as if doing a normal forward roll. This will bring your partner into a sitting position from which he can stand up. Now it's his turn to roll. Practise this until you can get a bit of speed up. Then try doing it backwards.

ACROBATICS/HEADSTAND

Headstands can be very useful stunts. You may remember Medici using a headstand in his cake-making routine, and you will find them very handy

for building the pyramid in the second half of this chapter.

To practise a headstand it's good to get a friend to hold your legs, or to practise against a wall, until you have got the hang of things. First kneel on the ground and place your hands on the ground in front of you, about a shoulder-width apart. Next place your forehead on the ground in front of your hands, so that your head and hands form an equal-sided triangle. Now straighten your legs and walk your feet forwards, until your weight is taken by your head and hands. Finally, slowly raise your legs off the ground. Keep them tucked in at first. When you feel balanced slowly straighten your legs.

The human spider

Put your arms around your friend's neck, jump up and wrap your legs around his waist. Hook your feet together so that you are quite secure. Now let go with your arms and bend over backwards (your partner should remain standing at this stage with his feet slightly apart). When you are upside down put your hands to the ground and 'walk' on them through your partner's legs. You should now be looking at the floor behind your partner. Your partner now bends forward and puts his hands on the floor. You can walk on six legs now – your partner's hands at the front, then his feet and then your hands.

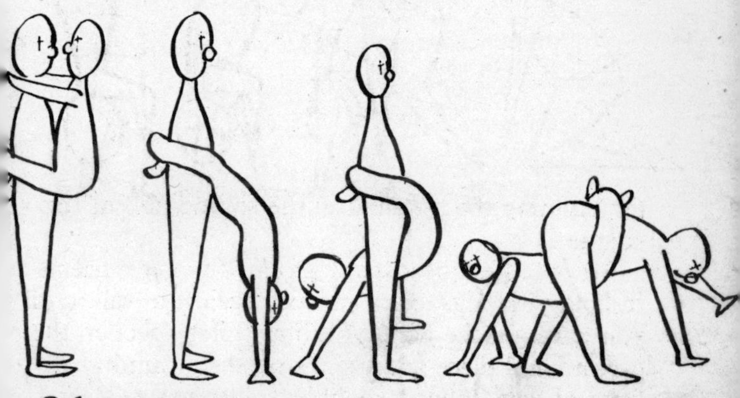

Other moves

If you do gymnastics at school then you probably know a whole range of other moves. Walkovers, cartwheels, round-offs, handsprings and back-flips would all make wonderful additions to any clown act.

PYRAMIDS

Pyramids are fun to build and not half as difficult as they look. They will add a really flashy touch to your show. As always put safety first, building the pyramids gradually, making sure everybody is comfortable in the position they have taken. Practise somewhere where there is a nice soft landing. Here are some pyramids you could try. How about designing your own?

Three-clown pyramid

Four-clown pyramid

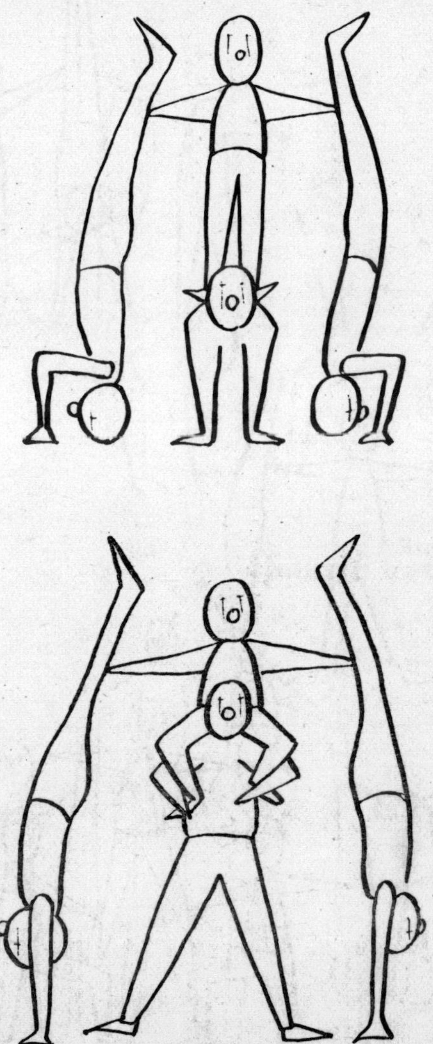

Five-clown pyramid

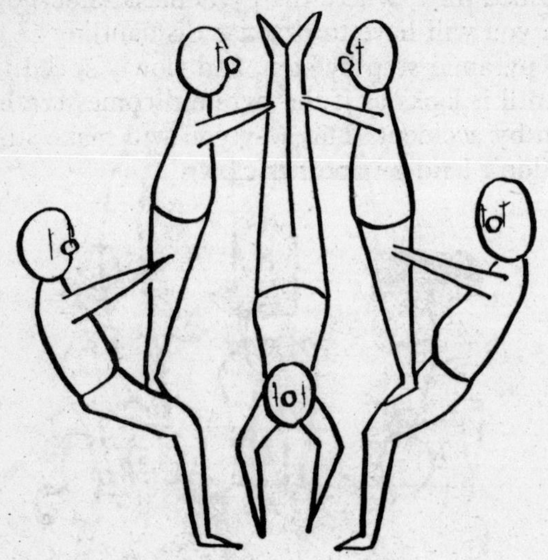

Ten-clown pyramid

If you are going to do a routine like the one described next, where the pyramid is knocked over, you will have to practise dismantling your pyramid step by step, and slowly speed it up until it looks as if the pyramid comes crashing down by accident. This way you will make sure you don't land on another clown.

ACROBATICS AND PYRAMIDS

Here we see the Great Medici's Clown Troupe performing an acrobatic act. Allsort, Cani, Loni, Grump and Mischievous Morris come on and build the magnificent five-man pyramid you see in the picture. Meanwhile Pierrot and Lorenzo start building a see-saw using a plank and a log. Medici announces that Pierrot is to stand on one end of this see-saw and be shot into space by Lorenzo jumping off his chair on to the other end.

Having completed three aerial somersaults Pierrot is to land on top of Morris's shoulders. Pierrot does a couple of cartwheels and walkovers to warm up, then stands on the end of the plank. With a cry Lorenzo jumps off his chair and into the air. He misses the plank, does a backward somersault and knocks over the pyramid. They all get up rubbing their bruised backs and behinds. Attempting to put things right Lorenzo gets out of his pocket a large bottle of medicine to rub into their aches and pains. Feeling a little better, they all go off, leaving Medici to announce the next act. He is halfway through when on rushes Morris calling for Lorenzo. Morris has doubled in height. From the other side comes Loni, who has shrunk to two feet. Finally Cani comes on. He has grown two extra legs.

Giant clowns

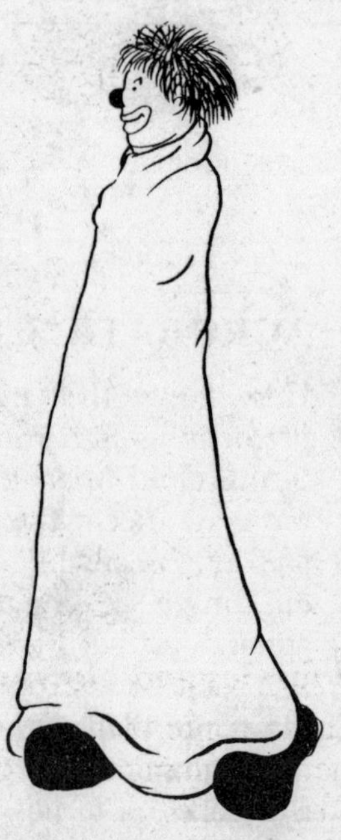

Morris turns himself into a giant by sitting on Grump's shoulders, and hiding him with a sheet.

Stand behind your partner, bend down and place your head between his legs, holding his knees with your hands. Then slowly stand up, keeping your back as straight as possible. Get your partner to hook his feet behind your shoulders. Now get someone to pass him up a big sheet to put over his shoulders to cover the two of you. This stunt is also very useful for building pyramids.

Midget clowns

To become a midget, Loni merely squats down and pulls the front of his jacket over his knees.

Four-legged clowns

Cani has not really grown two extra feet. Pierrot is merely walking right behind him, covered up by Cani's jacket.

6 JUGGLING

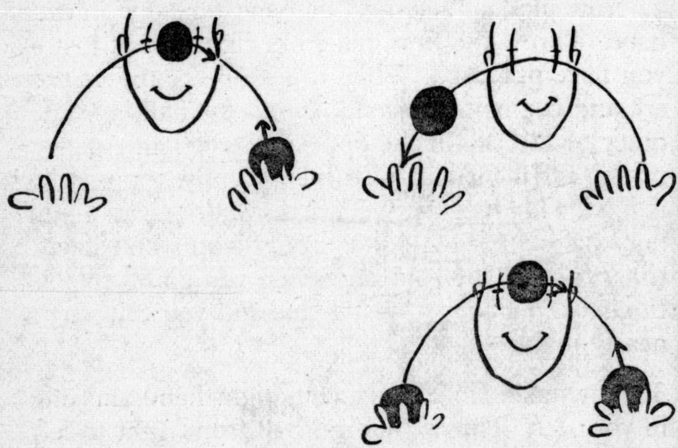

Juggling is a bit like riding a bicycle. Once you've learnt you will never forget. All the clowns in the Great Medici's Clown Troupe are keen jugglers. It may seem a bit tricky at first but it's worth having some patience, as once you have got the hang of it juggling is a real joy to do. Even if it turns out not to be the thing for you, have a look at the fake juggling routines on pages 77–78.

It is possible to juggle with just about anything, but before you attempt it with your mother's best dishes it's best to start with three balls. The heavier the balls the easier you will find them to catch. Solid rubber dog balls sold in pet shops are ideal.

To learn to juggle follow these three easy steps, mastering each one before going on to the next:

1. Pick up one ball, and practise throwing it from one hand to the other so that it makes a nice even arc, the top of which is level with your eyes. Practice this until you can do it without even looking at the ball.

2. Now pick up a second ball and take one in each hand. Throw the first ball from right to left just as you have practised. When it gets to the top of the arc and begins to descend, throw the ball in your other hand back in the opposite direction. Again make sure it forms a nice even arc, the top of which is level with your eyes. This is important as if you don't throw the ball high enough you won't have time to catch the next one when you go on to three-ball juggling. Master this and you can very nearly juggle.

3. Now take two balls in your right hand and one in your left. Throw the first ball from right to left and when it gets to the top of its arc release the ball in your left hand, as you have practised. When this second ball reaches the top of its arc throw the third ball. Then just keep going. Each time a ball gets to the top of its arc, throw the ball that is in the hand which is about to catch it. You are now a fully fledged juggler. After five throws stop and celebrate.

SOME GOLDEN TIPS

1. Never watch your hands catching the ball. Just concentrate on the point where the balls cross in front of your eyes.
2. Keep your shoulders relaxed and your wrists loose.

3. Direct the flight path of the balls with your fingers. Don't let your whole hand follow the direction of the ball.

Once you can juggle with three balls you can pop it in anywhere in your act. As you improve you can build up a more complicated routine. To give you an idea of what's possible the handbook now presents a juggling routine that Pierrot uses.

PIERROT'S SHOPPING-BASKET JUGGLING

Pierrot walks in looking a bit bored with life. He spots a shopping basket in the audience and picks it up to see what's inside. (In fact Pierrot placed it there before the show began.) First he takes out a paper bag with three apples in and starts juggling with these. Fancying the look of them he juggles with two in one hand and takes a bite out of the third one. He then goes on juggling, occasionally taking bites out of the apple till it has disappeared (known in the trade as the Disappearing Apple Routine).

Next he picks up a cauliflower, an orange and a peanut and juggles with these. Finally, looking wicked, he takes out a box of eggs and a sheet of newspaper. He lays the newspaper on the ground and starts juggling with the eggs.

After a bit he drops one on to the newspaper. Annoyed, he takes another egg, starts juggling, pretends to slip and hurls an egg into the audience. The audience scream as the egg comes flying towards them but there is no cause for alarm; it's a plastic one bought in a joke shop.

To finish his routine off Pierrot picks up the brown paper bag the apples were in, shows it to be empty, blows it up and pops it. Confetti flies everywhere. He puts everything back in the shopping bag, returns it to the audience and cartwheels off.

PHONEY JUGGLING

If you are too busy mastering other parts of your act to learn how to juggle, or are just feeling downright lazy, the piece of gadgetry below might come in handy. Although it will only fool the audience for a moment, it's a good comedy prop. Cani, who invented it, gets a laugh using it, then goes on to do some real juggling.

To make your phoney juggling apparatus you will need 2 metres of coathanger wire, black paint, a 15 cm piece of wood, some tape and three hollow rubber balls.

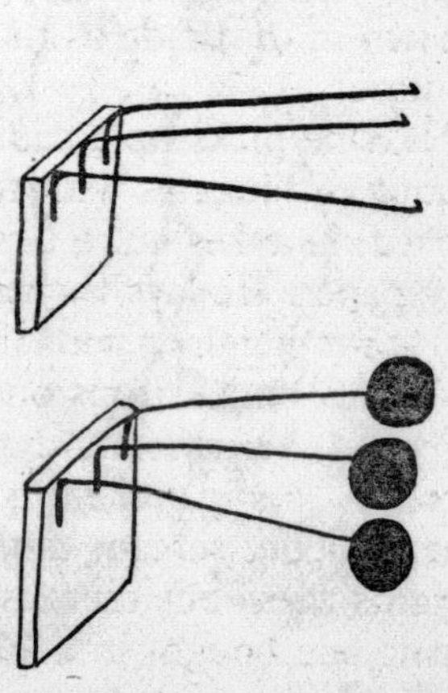

Cut your wire into three equal pieces and paint them black. Now bend these bits of wire as shown in the picture.

Next take your piece of wood and tape the pieces of wire on to it like this.

Finally, take the balls and pierce them with the ends of the wire. Your 'hooks' will keep them in place. You will end up with something like this.

All you have to do now is stick the piece of wood down the front of your trousers, so that the three pieces of wire protrude over the top of the waist-band as shown in this picture of Morris. If you knock the balls up and down with your hands it will look for a moment as if you are doing a dazzlingly fast juggling display. It will take the audience longer to spot the pieces of wire if you wear a dark shirt and jacket. Walk on to the stage juggling and as the audience gape in wonder take a bow with your hands behind your back, the three balls magically suspended in front of you.

BOOK-CATCHING

Another fiendish piece of cheating based on the same principle as the phoney juggling gadgetry, this one really will fool your audience.

In this act Morris walks on stage, holding a book out in front by squeezing it between two other books.

He pauses a moment, musters up every bit of concentration he can find and with a cry whips away the two books he is holding, and before the middle one falls to the ground, he catches it again from the top and bottom.

As the audience marvel, back and forth Morris flies catching the middle book at all sorts of different angles. Finally he tries to go too fast and drops a book. He bends forward to pick it up. The middle book hangs suspended in mid air.

How's it done? Just the same way as the phoney juggling except that, this time, one book is fixed to a wire: Morris holds the other two.

7 COSTUME

Now is the moment for big decisions. This chapter will tell you how to make anything from top hats, Pierrot costumes and bald heads to big feet, bulbous noses and squirting flowers. As you can't wear everything, you must first decide what sort of clown you want to be.

This chapter describes how each clown in the Medici troupe went about making his outfit. But of course you don't have to copy them. You could wear a top hat like Medici, a jacket and roll-up tie like Cani and a big pair of shoes like Lorenzo's, or come up with some brilliant ideas of your own. Your choice of costume will, of course, depend on what sort of acts you fancy performing. If you are a bit of an acrobat, big feet could be very troublesome. The best thing to do is experiment until you feel just right in your costume.

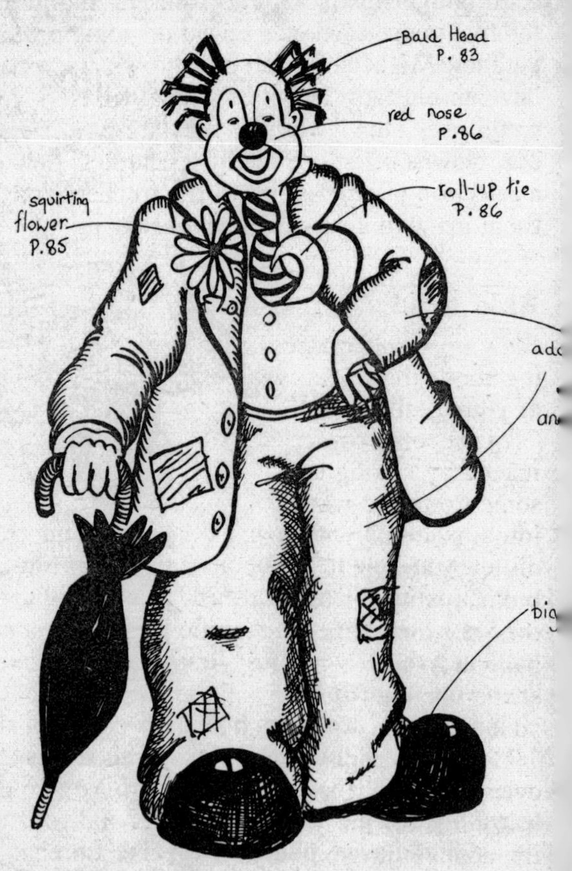

CANI'S COSTUME

Cani's costume is a classic Auguste clown's get-up. Even if you don't want to be an Auguste clown, you may still want to borrow some ideas from his costume and props.

Adapted trousers and jackets

Cani bought his jacket and trousers in a jumble sale for five pence each and sewed on some nice bright patches. Might your dad or a grown-up you know have an old tatty jacket or pair of trousers you could use? Don't worry if they are five sizes too big, clowns often use ill-fitting clothes. Sew or glue a selection of patches on to the trousers and hold them up with a pair of braces or string.

Bald head

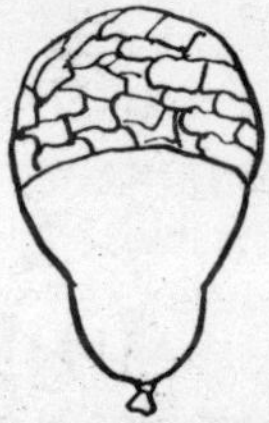

Blow up a balloon until it's about the same size as your head.

Make some papier mâché by mixing up some flour and water into a paste. Dip strips of newspaper in this and build them up in layers over the top of the balloon until you get a shape like the top of your head.

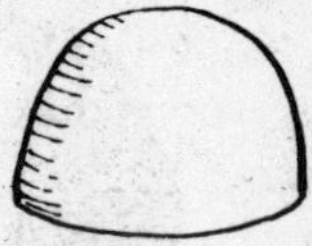

Leave the paper to dry overnight. Burst the balloon and trim round the edge. Paint your bald head to match your make-up. If you want it glossy you can varnish it.

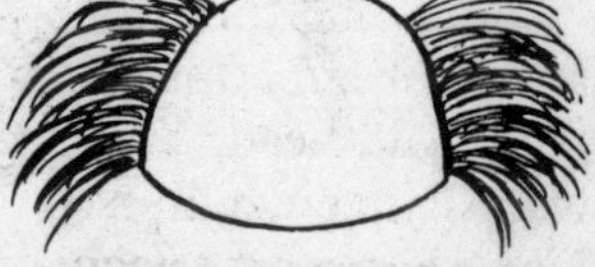

If you want to attach some hair, make a fringe, as described in the next section, and glue it around the edge. Alternatively you could use bits of cotton wool, straw or shredded paper.

False hair

If you would like some hair on your bald head, here's what to do.

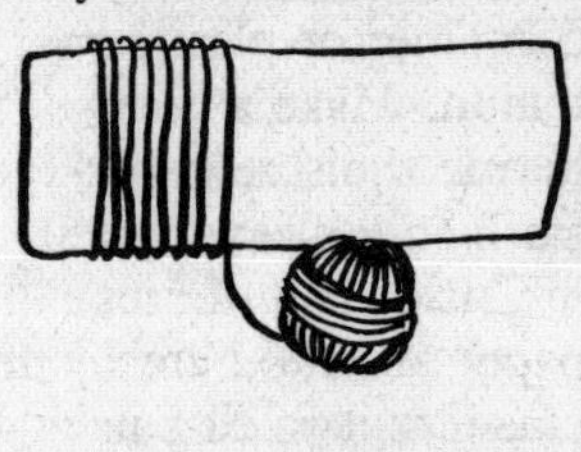

Cut a strip of card long enough to go around the bald head. If you want the hair to be long cut a wide piece of card (about 25 to 30 cm) or if you want short hair cut a narrow piece of card (about 10 cm).

Wind wool around the card, working your way from one end of the card to the other.

Stick the wool together along one side with sticky tape, or better still stitch along the wool making sure you catch each strand.

Cut the wool along the other side. The card should come away.

Now glue the fringe around the bottom of your bald head. Your wool fringe would also look very good attached to the bottom of a hat.

Squirting flowers

Get a plastic sauce container or plastic lemon. Make a hole beside the screw top. Push in a plastic straw.

Cut a strip of crêpe paper about 32 cm by 4 cm. Cut it so that it stretches lengthways.

Fold it up like this and cut out a petal shape – don't cut the bottom two corners.

Open up the paper. Glue along the bottom edge and roll the 'petals' around the top of the straw. Do not block the end of the straw.

Carefully stretch out each petal to make a flower.

Fill the lemon with water and put it in your top pocket so that the flower pokes out over the top. When your target comes within range, press your top pocket and fire.

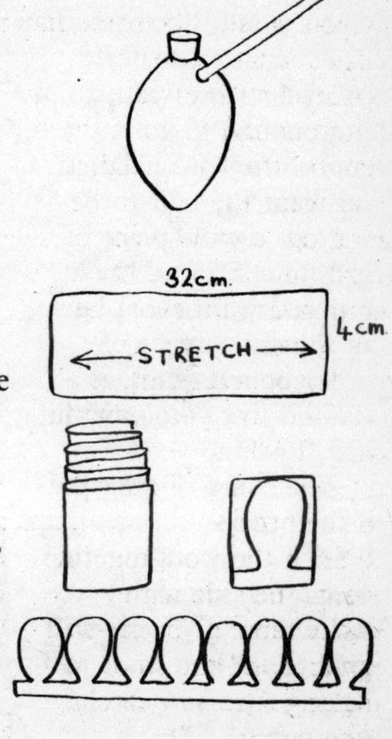

Roll-up tie

Get a plastic washing-up liquid bottle or similar container and wash it out thoroughly. Cut off the top and bottom with a pair of scissors.

Now cut out a line spiralling around the remaining tube of plastic, as shown.

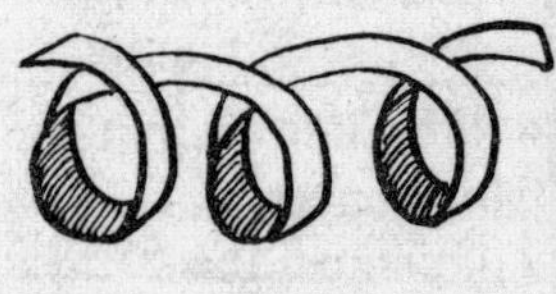

If you stretch it, it should give you something like this.

Now start feeding the end of the spiral of plastic into the end of your tie. Cut it off when you have fed in enough. This will give you a first-class roll-up tie.

Noses

Cut a ping-pong ball in half, or use the 'bump' from an egg carton. Trim it so it doesn't pinch your nose. Punch breathing holes. Thread thin elastic through either side to go around your head. Paint your false nose a nice bright red.

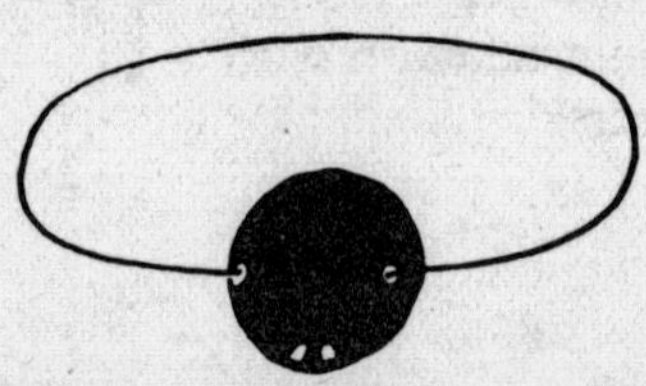

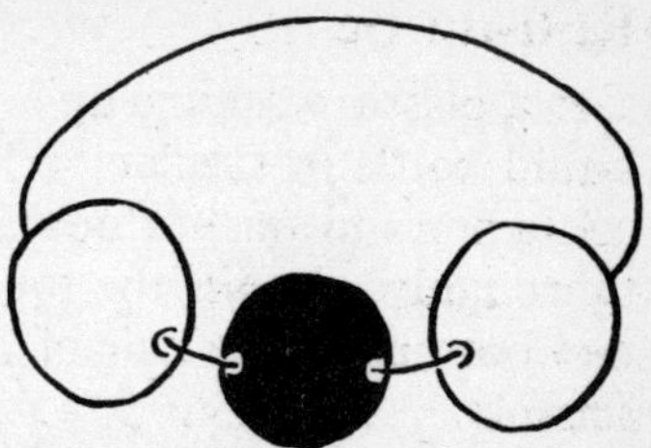

Nose with cheeks

Use two halves of a ping-pong ball, or small rubber ball. Paint them to match your make-up and thread them on the elastic either side of the false nose.

PIERROT'S COSTUME

Pierrot has one of the most distinctive and elegant of all costumes. Like his make-up, Pierrot's costume is all black and white. It is surprisingly easy to make but you will need to find yourself an old sheet.

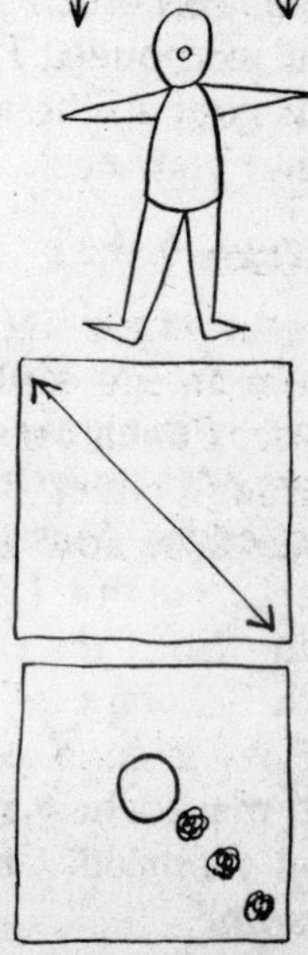

Measure yourself from one wrist to the other.

Cut a sheet into a square so that the length from each opposite corner is the same as your arm measurement.

Cut a hole in the middle of the square just big enough for your head to go through. Stick or sew two or three pom-poms down the front.

This should be worn with white trousers.

Pierrot's frill

Get a piece of elastic which, when the ends are tied together, will fit fairly closely round your neck, but will stretch easily over your head.

Cut a piece of white crêpe paper about 1 metre long and about 30 cm wide. Fold it in half lengthways. Stretch it along the open edge.

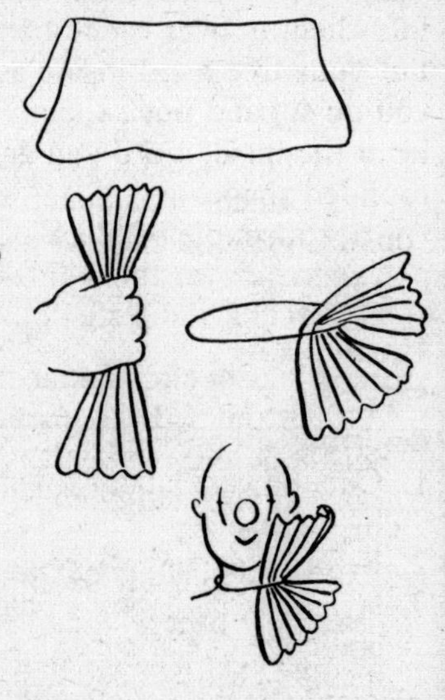

Unfold it, gather it up together and push it halfway through the elastic.

Fold the bunched-up paper in half over the elastic.

Put this over your head and pull the paper so it goes all the way round your neck.

Pierrot's hat

Get a piece of card, about 50 cm by 60 cm. Roll it into a cone by bringing one of the short edges over to one of the long edges. Make sure it overlaps about 1.5 cm at the point. Stick the edges together with Sellotape.

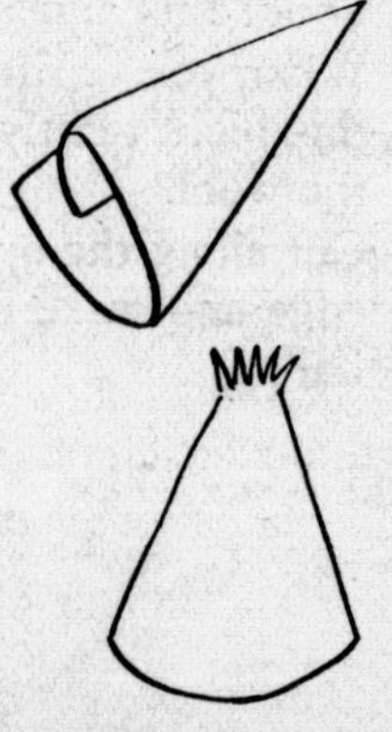

Put the cone on your head and mark where it fits on your forehead. Cut around this line.

To get the rounded top, snip all around the point several times. Make your cuts about 5 cm long.

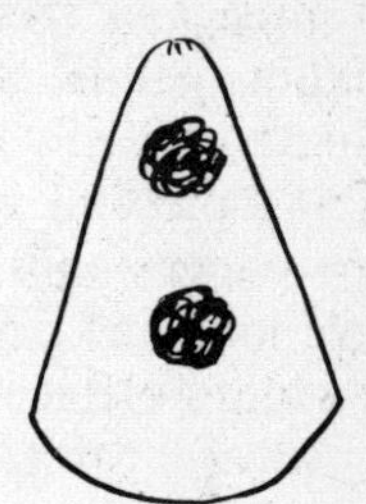

Put glue on these tabs and fold them in over each other. Put your free hand inside as you do so, and push them from the inside until you get a rounded shape.

Stick a couple of black pom-poms down the front.

Pom-poms

Make your pom-poms in the same way as the fringe described on page 84. But:

1. Cut the card about 4 cm by 4 cm.
2. Before you start winding, lay a length of wool along one edge of the card. Then wind the wool over it. Wind the wool around about fifty times.
3. When you've finished, tie this piece tightly round the wool.
4. Cut along the opposite edge and make it into a ball.

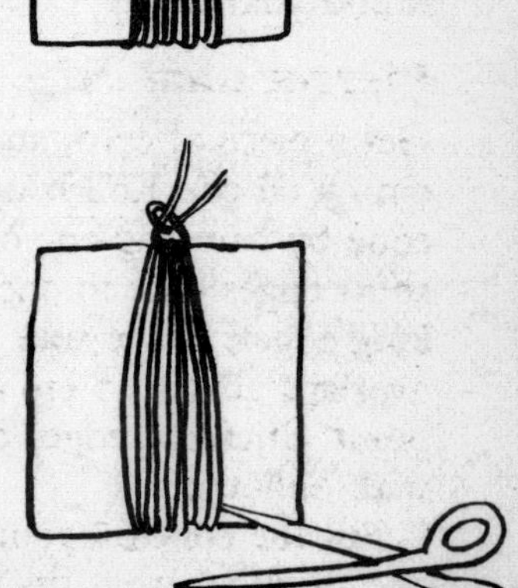

LORENZO'S COSTUME

Lorenzo wears a bald head and spectacles, a costume similar to Pierrot's and a pair of giant feet.

Spectacles

For this you need two lengths of lightweight wire, each about 45 cm long, and one piece about 3 cm long. Shape the two long pieces like this.

Then attach the two wire circles in the middle using the short piece.

Instant disguise kit

Attach a false nose, eyebrows and moustache to the spectacles like this. (See page 95 for false moustaches.)

Giant feet

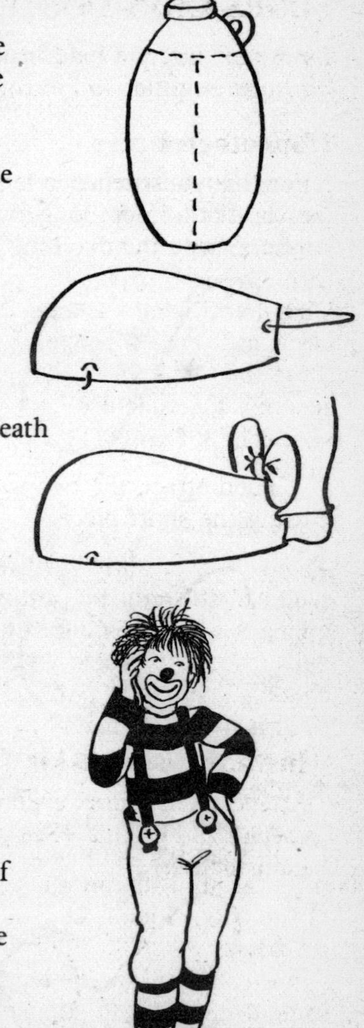

Get a large plastic bottle or container. Cut off the top and then cut it in half lengthways.

Punch two holes at the top ends of each half. Thread through some elastic or string to put round the back of your ankles to hold them in place. You may need another piece of elastic threaded around underneath your shoes.

Paint them and stick a nice big bow on each. Now try doing the hokey-kokey!

MORRIS'S COSTUME

Morris wears a stripy tee-shirt, a pair of trousers held up with braces and folded up at the bottom, and a pair of stripy coloured socks. All these you might have in a drawer at home. Dungarees are also good clowning gear.

LONI'S COSTUME

Loni is distinctive for his fine hooped trousers and his huge bow tie.

Hooped trousers

Unpick a few stitches in the waistband of your trousers and thread through some coathanger wire. Bend it into a large circle as it goes through. Tape the two ends securely together. Re-stitch the bit you've unpicked.

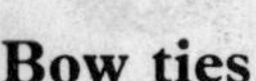

Bow ties

Make a big brightly coloured bow tie using fabric (you can stiffen it by putting Sellotape on it or by giving it a thin coating of paste) or crêpe paper.

Cut out a rectangle about 40 cm by 10 cm. Fold it like this. Then squeeze it together in the middle.

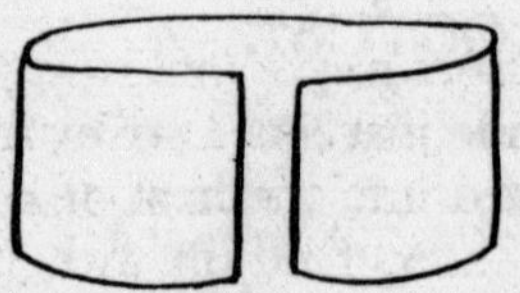

Cut another rectangle about 5 cm by 2 cm and roll it around the middle of the bow. Stick it at the back.

Fasten your bow tie to some thin elastic to go round your neck.

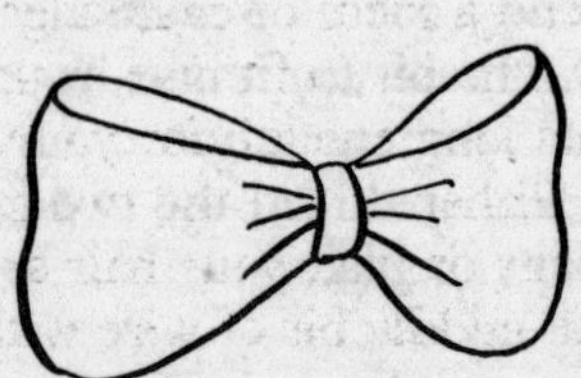

ALLSORT'S COSTUME

Allsort wears stand-up pigtails, a hooped dress, made just like Loni's trousers but with the wire fitted into the hem of her dress, and tights.

How to make your pigtails stand to attention

Bend a piece of coathanger wire like this, the middle bit to fit over your head and the two end bits long enough for your plaits.

Either thread the two end bits through your plaits or plait your hair around them. Camouflage the middle bit of wire with ribbon, and tie big bows to the ends of your plaits.

GRUMP'S COSTUME

A tramp's costume like Grump's is one of the easiest costumes of all to assemble. Grump wears a tatty old raincoat that looks as if it's been stored in a puddle, a hat that seems to have been trampled on by a herd of elephants, a pair of old frayed, patched trousers and hob-nailed boots.

THE GREAT MEDICI'S COSTUME

Medici's glories are his top hat and his moustache.

Top hats

Get a sheet of cardboard about 30 cm by 60 cm, and wrap it around your forehead to give you a tube of card the size of your head. Stick the edges together.

To make the top of your hat, place the tube of card on to another piece of card, trace around the edge and cut out the circle.

To make the brim, draw another circle, 5 cm wider, around the hole you will now have in your card and cut around the outer edge of this.

Now take your tube of card and cut zig-zags along the top and bottom as in the picture. Bend the top ones inward. Fit your circle of card on top and glue them together. Now slide your brim on to the other end. Bend the zig-zags outward so they support the brim, and glue.

Moustaches

To create a magnificent moustache like Medici's either trim a wool fringe (see page 84) to the shape you want, or lay some strands of wool together and simply tie them in the middle. You can keep your moustache in shape by stiffening it with paste or glue. Stick it on to your face.

8 MAKE-UP

A clown's make-up is one of his most distinguishing and important features. You will have to become an expert at putting your make-up on, so read this section thoroughly before experimenting to see what sort of face suits you best. Although different families of clowns wear similar make-up, every clown will have his own unique, individual face.

WHAT TO USE

Bought make-up

The trouble with bought make-up is that it's very expensive. If this doesn't put you off then most joke or fancy-dress hire shops sell clown make-up kits including white base and several colours. Otherwise ask for 'white pancake' and a couple of 'sticks' of colour.

Home-made make-up

If you mix powder paint with baby lotion you can create your own exclusive brand of make-up. You can choose any colour you like, and it has the advantage of being easy to wash off. For your black lines burn the end of a cork with a match and then rub the matchstick through the soot. This will give you your very own black liner pencil. Many clowns still use this method for making black make-up.

GOLDEN TIPS

1. Always be near soap, water and a mirror.
2. Keep tissues handy for wiping make-up off hands.
3. Put an old sheet over you to protect your costume.
4. Wash your face before starting.

AUGUSTE CLOWNS

Although there are no hard and fast rules about make-up, Auguste clowns often have big brightly coloured hoops above their faces and a big red mouth like Cani. When putting these on your face it's best to draw the outline with a little make-up on a matchstick, and then colour them in with the

tip of your finger. Some clowns cover their whole faces with white make-up first. If you do this let it dry before putting the colours on top. These colours should be nice and bright; reds, yellows and greens work very well. You will also need to make yourself a nice big nose (as described in the chapter on costumes).

TRAMP CLOWNS

The most distinctive feature of tramp clowns is their stubbly, unshaven look. To create this effect take your cork and rub the burnt end over your chin and jaw line. Use a nice big red nose and red mouth to add a bit of colour.

PIERROT CLOWNS

Pierrot clowns wear no colour in their make-up. First put on a white base all over your face. Then take your matchstick, or a toothpick if you want the ideal tool, and rub it on the burnt cork. For the straight black lines through the eyes lay the edge of your stick on to your face, first below then above the eye. This is easier than trying to draw the lines free-hand. To make the eyes more expressive also draw lines round the edge of the eye itself. Do this

very carefully, looking up at the ceiling as you draw under your eyes and closing them when putting on the line along the eyelid.

OTHER CLOWNS

Mischievous Morris, Medici and Lorenzo all use combinations of these traditional make-ups. Morris uses the Auguste clowns' big red lips and nose but wears no make-up round the eyes. Medici adopts Pierrot make-up, and adds a grand-looking moustache.

REGISTERING YOUR FACE

For hundreds of years clowns have 'registered' their faces by painting them on empty eggshells. How about doing this, so if you become famous one day a museum could have a copy of your original make-up design? Paint the eggshell with water colours or poster paint. To make a really posh job of it, varnish it afterwards.

TAKING MAKE-UP OFF

'Pancake' make-up and your baby-lotion recipe should wash off with soap and water. Grease-based make-up should be removed with tissues and removing cream or baby lotion. Be careful taking the make-up off from around your eyes. A sponge is best for this.

MAKE-UP KIT

Keep your make-up and everything else you need, such as tissues, a small mirror, matchsticks and your cork, in a special make-up box and keep everything in good order. Small tool-boxes make ideal make-up boxes but a shoe-box will do the job well.

9 THE HISTORY OF CLOWNS

If you are a clown who is taking his trade seriously you may want to know a little more about your clown ancestors, the different traditions of clowning and their history.

Clowns have been around a long time. Five thousand years ago the Egyptians had clowns, called *dangas*, who would be sent to amuse Pharaohs, when they were feeling down and feeding too many people to the crocodiles.

Pierrot, Lorenzo and Medici all have distant relations who were Commedia dell'Arte clowns, perhaps the most famous troupes of all time. These clown troupes, who began travelling and performing their shows in Italy over 500 years ago, had their own clowns' handbooks full of *lazzi*, their name for routines. The books were full of slapstick sequences, stunts, jokes and other business and are the basis for much of the material in this more up-to-date handbook.

The Commedia dell'Arte clowns toured all over Europe and performed to rich and poor alike, in market places and royal palaces, streets and theatres.

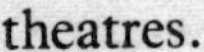

Cani and Loni are Auguste clowns and have their background in the circus. About 200 years ago there was an acrobat and juggler called Tom Belling who was working for a German circus. Tom Belling was in big trouble with the circus boss, Herr Renz, and trying to hide from him, disguised himself in a red wig and a large jacket turned inside out. Trying to make his escape he bumped straight into his boss

and panicked. He backed through the curtains into the ring, and fell over a rope. He stood up and promptly slipped over again. The audience, thinking it was a new act, loved it and laughed and applauded calling out, 'Auguste! Auguste!' which meant 'clumsy idiot' in the local language. Tom backed out through the curtains, but Herr Renz, delighted with the audience's reaction, pushed him back into the ring telling him to keep going. So began a famous clowning career. Ever since then clowns have copied Tom's manner of dress and are still called 'Auguste' to this day.

Grump comes from America, where the tramp clown was made famous by Charlie Chaplin and first introduced to the circus by a sad old tramp figure named Emmet Kelly, who became much loved by people all over the world.

Allsort is the most recent kind of clown in the Medici Troupe. Once upon a time it was not thought proper for women to perform as clowns but today some of the most famous clowns are women.

And last but not least we come to Mischievous Morris Malloy. Morris's ancestors were jesters who date back to the times of Richard the Lionheart, Henry VIII and Elizabeth I, all of whom, like their subjects, had jesters. In a time when there were no televisions, films or radios, and few books, the jesters had a busy time keeping people amused, telling jokes and stories, doing juggling and acrobatics. They had a very special place in the land, being the only people who were able to criticize and mock the king and his lords without having their heads removed.

If you want to know more about clowns, you should be able to find a book about them in your local library.

10 PUTTING ON YOUR SHOW

If you have organized your costume, designed your make-up and worked on your routines, then the big moment has arrived and you are ready to take to the stage and stun the world with the wonders of your show. Before booking the local football stadium it is probably best to begin by trying out your show at home for friends and family. The Great Medici began his career performing to his pet gerbil and three goldfish, and it was only their unbridled enthusiasm that persuaded him to try his act on a wider audience.

If your show goes well practise some more and then consider where else you could perform, at school, or friends' parties, at playschemes or playgrounds, for the people in your street or at the local park. The possibilities are endless.

STAGING

A clown show can be performed just about anywhere there is room for you to perform your act and fit the audience in. If there is a lot of pie- and water-flinging slapstick in your show, you will need somewhere which will not be permanently scarred by your turning it into a battlefield of mucky missiles. These shows are usually best staged outside.

You will of course need somewhere to enter and exit from. The best solution is to make your own clown's 'backdrop'. Otherwise you will need to use a door into another room, or (say) the back of a shed, or a gate in a fence if you are in the garden.

Making a backcloth

Having your own backcloth will add a real touch of class to your show as well as giving you something to store your props behind. Get a large double sheet or dust sheet and write the name of your show or troupe on it. Even better, dye it first. If one of you is a good artist you could paint a picture or scene on the front. Poster paint with a little

wallpaper paste mixed in will do the job very well. Now hang the backdrop using string or poles and guy ropes.

REHEARSALS

Write down all the routines you could use in your show. Now work them out in the order in which they appear. Try and think of ways of opening the show, and a really effective finale. Make sure you have practised all your routines, and then have a couple of run-throughs to make sure everything is working right. Finally have a dress rehearsal and perform the show just as if there really was an audience sitting there.

You are now ready for your audience.

GETTING AN AUDIENCE

If you are performing for friends and families you can just invite them along. But if you are doing a show at school or in the park you could advertise it by making some posters. Write or paint these on to large pieces of paper or card. Advertise the name of your show, where it's to take place and when. Could you paint on some clowns, or a scene from one of your acts?

SHOWTIME

Get organized well before your audience arrives and know exactly what you have to do. If you have practised hard and really got to know your handbook you should have a hum-dinger of a show, which will have your audience rolling in the aisles and be a first step to fame and fortune. Good luck and

BON VOYAGE

A GHOST HUNTER'S HANDBOOK

Peter Underwood

Long-time ghost expert and hunter, Peter Underwood, tells children all they need to know about ghosts, their habits and habitats. Peter Underwood, who is president of the Ghost Club and copyright holder of the only known photograph of a ghost, has written several books on ghosts for adults, but this is his first book on the subject for children. Serious in approach, it covers everything from how to find a ghost to information on ghosts that have been found in all parts of the world, and includes a section on famous ghosts and haunted houses that can be visited.

85p

THE SPARROW BOOK OF RECORD-BREAKERS

Pamela Cleaver

Children have flown planes in the RAF, ridden in cavalry charges and formed an army in which the eldest soldier was twelve years old. A young boy was used as a spy in World War Two, and the youngest author to have a book published was only four and a half years old.

And that is only the beginning . . .

85p